Just

Faith

It!

FADRIENNE JONES

Just

Faith

It!

Just FAITH It!

Published in 2022 by

Seven Door Multimedia Beverly Hills, CA 90211.

Library of Congress Cataloging-in-Publications-Data

Unless otherwise indicated, Scripture quotations are from the Amplified or King James Version of the Holy Bible. (Via Biblegateway.com) All rights reserved.

Printed in the United States of America

10 9 8 7 6 5 4 3 2 1

Introduction

Have you ever been running late to a meeting, or a dinner reservation and you finally get out of the door, and into the car, only to get stuck in traffic? And if getting stuck in traffic isn't enough, you get behind someone who is preoccupied with something such as their phone, causing you to move at an even slower pace. The worst thing ever, right? It's not like that person doesn't have the potential to move faster, they're just choosing to place their focus and attention on something other than getting through traffic at a steady pace. Throughout my life, I've met several people who were not focused, causing them to not operate at their potential therefore preventing their life from moving at a much faster pace than it could.

There is nothing worse than unrealized or wasted potential. We all have the potential to become whatever we desire, but unfortunately not everyone utilizes that opportunity. There are also those who would love to realize their potential but need a little help in doing so. Let me ask you a question: if you are reading this book, have you maximized your potential? If yes, how can you improve? If no, what are you waiting for? The right time? To have enough money? To have supporters?

But we've all had moments that are nothing more than time stealers. Moments where you're extremely motivated, and then moments of despair that send you pummeling into the abyss of stagnation, and if you're honest...depression. Moments that make you feel as if you can climb the highest mountain, and then moments that make you feel as though you have permanent address in the lowest of valleys.

These varying moments that come with or without warning, can convince you that you are teetering along the edges of insanity, or stuck in a pit that you'll never be able to crawl your way out of. As I began to ponder the "why" to this book, my mind traveled down the corridors of time, and I thought about every time I found myself stuck between where I wanted to be and where I was. Isn't it crazy how easy it is to see the dream or the desired goal, but how difficult it is to realize or reach it? One day you can have the perfect plan and the next day, it all seems impossible.

This book is for the person who is tired of dreaming. Tired of waiting for the perfect moment. Tired of wondering if someone is going to open the door for you. Tired of trying to figure out if you have what it takes to make it big, or what it takes to go all of the way. This book is for the person who sits in the middle of the bed, surrounded by papers and sticky notes that contain the roadmap to your destiny, but never move past the planning stage to the DO IT stage. This book is for the person who has decided they are tired of procrastinating and are ready to throw caution to the wind and LEAP!

Chapter One

I'm Not Where I Want to Be

If one is going to be happy in their life, they must learn the art of patience. No one sails through life without docking on the shores of patience a time or two. Patience is an essential part of the bedrock of happiness because you must quickly understand that sometimes life doesn't always pan out the way we think it will, or the way we think it should. Having patience will allow you to accept those changes without having a pessimistic attitude about things you cannot control. If things are not going the way you want them to, instead of getting frustrated, you must learn to be patient. You need to see things and situations in a positive light to make your life happier.

To get that positivity, you need to be patient. If you find any life situation challenging, or find it difficult to bear, try to re-frame that situation and see its positive side. To say patience is a virtue is an understatement. It's really more of a skill—one that can be learned and needs constant nurturing. Patience is the state of being that occurs between experience and reaction. Whether you're trying to be patient with yourself, others, or life, it seems to always involve the experience of dealing with delays or obstacles. By cultivating a practice of patience, you're able to let go of things outside your control and live with less stress, anxiety, and frustration. It's not an easy practice, but here are a few perspectives on how to cultivate patience to open up new possibilities that will propel you to your next level.

When you look at what it means to have patience, you're ultimately talking about dealing with your own thoughts and emotions. As a spiritual being there is an unbounded, limitless presence within you that is constantly seeking expression. You think, act, and experience, and this should be the simplicity of life. Unfortunately, it's not that simple. Problems arise when what you think and do doesn't seem to produce immediate results. Maybe it's time to look inward and ask why you don't have patience with yourself.

Ask yourself:

- What does it mean to be patient with myself?
- What benefits would I experience by being patient with myself?
- What can I do to become more patient with myself?

Remember that patience is the ability to not be troubled by life's changes, delays, or other undesirables. It's the ability to maintain stillness in the midst of disappointment.

Try to practice self-awareness in those moments where you feel the greatest need for patience.

- Pay attention to what arises in you
- Notice where you feel the stress
- Listen to your thoughts
- Take note of your emotions

A powerful benefit to practicing patience is that you cultivate the peace of mind to guide yourself out of these moments. Even the simple act of looking within at a time when you're feeling impatient can be healing. Use awareness to maintain your calm. Tap into your stillness and preserve it. See these moments of self-reflection as opportunities to strengthen yourself in self-control and grace. I know you may be reading that thinking it is so much easier said than done. I feel you. But, hey, change doesn't happen overnight anyway.

I transformed from being pessimistic to optimistic when I became weary of getting the same results. I once believed that if I anticipated the worst, I could guard myself against disappointments. If I could survive the walls caving in around me, then that was the best I could expect. Focusing on nothing more than the less didn't amount to anything at all in my eyes because without even realizing it, this became my ceiling, and nothing went beyond that limit. Before reaching my breaking point, or shall I say awakening, I used to ask myself, "How would things get better? What am I doing wrong?" Then, it hit me like a ton of bricks. "Fadrienne, you're more negative than anything else." So, I started to observe my words and actions towards other people. I became more aware of how I was perceived, my actions, my energy, my vibe, my attitude, and my outlook on life Above all else, I became sensitive towards self. I began to explore areas of my heart and character.

I often reflect on people like T.D. Jakes, Oprah Winfrey, and Joel Olsteen (just to name a few), and how they incorporate positive messages, as well as their personal lives. Their message of hope seems to illuminate from within and touching everyone in their path. Thus, always remarkable. When I hear their messages, I tell myself, "That's what I want be—a hope dealer." Because it was seen on television, I thought it was a career. However, I soon discovered it's a lifestyle, and with any transition, it needs things daily to grow. As I stated earlier, patience is very important because it should be a person's foundation or anchor. It takes time to understand how to apply the brakes on what we may perceive as urgent. If an individual press too early, he or she will feel the need to get caught up before it spins out of control. If a person applies too late, then he or she will over think the situation. Therefore, leaving him or her vulnerable to panic attacks. This trait is critical because it should be a person's foundation or anchor.

For instance, for some odd reason, I had programmed myself into believing that everything had to be instant or else it wouldn't happen. For most of us, we desire to be wealthy so we can be celebrated by others who have already arrived to the top. I'm sure you can attest there have been many days and nights of frustration as you've worked to get to the level you want to be. You don't have to tell me, but I know there have been days you wanted to give up. But, when you are building an empire, the option to give up shouldn't be an option at all. I retrospectively look back to how I have rushed people to get things done in a hurry, and ninety-five percent of the time it never turned out right because I didn't allow the necessary time it took for situations to properly unfold.

Speaking of, I will pause to say that cultivating patience with others is an entirely different challenge. Other people are always acting, thinking, and feeling in ways that are potentially disagreeable. Since everyone has a right to personal freedom, no one has the right to hinder others from their life or personal self-expression—no matter how much you'd like to sometimes. It's hard to simply live and let live. The problem with this is that you're constantly surrounded by other people and the ways you live your life will be different. The gift of living through patience, however, is that you become less reactionary. When others let you down or irritate you, be patient with them. Gently express love and stillness. Remember that they are growing—just like you—and that life is a process. Whatever issues you may have with another person are more than likely temporary and will undoubtedly change once you let go of your own agenda. What disturbs you now about this person may change and in the next moment you may laugh with them or feel some other positive emotion. Regardless of what other people do or think, you have a choice in how you allow it to affect you. Your mind may jump to negative notions and reactions, your body may even register a response, but you are the source of it all. Ultimately you can tap into your stillness, your peace. Remember this and from this have patience. You are one with the eternal. The things, people, and situations in your life change. Patience is an expression of this awareness and of love.

Once I implemented patience towards all aspects of my life, (time is a key factor), I noticed a considerable change with everything. Time not only reveals how good things come to those who wait but also by moving slowly, I can see the bigger picture and make adjustments accordingly. Therefore, this valuable lesson has helped me recognize when I become eager or anxious about something new, the understanding of how to apply the brakes kick in towards what I may perceive as urgent. Before my transformation, pressing too early was truly a lifestyle.

Gaining patience can be transformative to your overall life experience. So much of life is about awareness, growth, and learning—these are the things that are always going on behind the scenes. When you want things to happen in your life, you can prolong the process by giving your attention and energy to the frustration you feel about waiting. The waiting is not the problem. It's how you deal with it, how you see it. Practicing patience shifts your attention away from the stress and frustration. Acting with patience is a way of telling life that you are in charge. You are in no hurry, there is no distress—only peace and confidence in your truth. This is an imperial trait—one of strength and majesty over your life's circumstances.

Practicing patience will help you dissipate stress and give you a choice about how you respond to disappointment and frustration. When you can stay calm, centered and not act rashly out of frustration, all areas of your life will improve, and you will have the main ingredient needed to truly GO through life.

Chapter Two

Mirror, Mirror On the Wall

Have you ever examined your personal narrative? What stories do you tell yourself about yourself? Have you ever considered that some of those stories might not be true? Have you ever examined where the stories you tell yourself about yourself came from and continue to come from?

Here are a few places where the stories of ourselves come from: things our parents said; things our teachers said; things our peers said; things people we dated said; things our spouses say or said; comparisons we make between who we think we are and what we think we should be; stories we have created and believed in order to protect our fragile egos (and many of these stories can be, oddly, self-hating stories). Given the intensity and number of stories that we have internalized about ourselves, how can we ever see ourselves clearly and finally be honest with ourselves?

Being honest with yourself is a daily, hourly, even by-the-minute practice. The practice is being conscious of what we're doing and asking ourselves why we're doing it. At any given moment, what story are you telling yourself? Especially in moments of difficulty, being honest with yourself means separating yourself from your personal narrative. Can you step back from the running story of your life that runs through your head? To step away from the story, we must step into something/somewhere else. Being real — being truly honest with yourself — happens when we focus completely on something outside ourselves. When we become so immersed in something that our idea of who we are exits the premises, is when honesty with ourselves is possible.

Being honest with yourself is not so common as it turns out we are blatant liars. Just listen to that inner dialogue without filtering for once. My turning point not just in my career but in my life, came when I got uncomfortably honest with myself. In other words, when I was telling all the truth. It does not matter that I did not do anything about it for a little while. I had taken that first step. I had stopped lying and started telling the truth to myself – not to the outside world, forget them for a minute please – but to YOURSELF.

Do you know what it's like to have that inner dialogue with your ego, to give up the pursuit of the only thing that you thought would make you "successful" after all the years of investment and sacrifice? Not a pretty day, yet it liberates you from the sham and drudgery of lying to your beautiful soul. I say that's worth it.

In those first moments of allowing the honesty and letting your heart whisper, "Honey, this nonsense isn't for you! It's OK. You can start over. Enough betraying your heart!", it's all you can do to keep breathing and not hyperventilate. This stuff is not easy but let me tell you a secret: Easy sucks. Easy is over-rated. Easy for the lazy part of you that you need to eradicate. Easy gives your soul a virus. Easy is the pits. Easy is the road to misery. You need to forget about easy versus hard and stop whining about it. Your job, after you get honest with yourself, is to ask how and start figuring it out one step at a time.

Honesty comes with other issues too. Honesty brings you face to face with some ugly resistance first. I could not separate my identity from my dream; I am my dream, I am my career, I am my company. I am meant to go down this path. I am not meant to go down the path of uncertainty. Complete resistance. So, stop resisting. Yes, that's as simple as it is. I am not trying to be cute or clever. Just stop resisting. Have you even tried? Stop resisting and go with the flow of that honesty. You won't die, I promise!

There is a good side to honesty, and this might comfort you. Changing what you know to be the only "truth" to listen to your soul is terrifying, and that's all you want to focus on because your mind wants you to resist the change, but if you pay attention, in all that fear and commotion, you will feel a little peace.

In the end of your life, whoever you are, you won't give a damn anymore anyway and then you will be utterly honest with yourself. Why not start sooner and actually do something about the divine message of honesty? Honesty liberates you from your rules. It lifts heavy, ugly weight off your shoulders and maybe in that weight, you also store some good stuff, that's okay. Let them come off. Maybe you stored your security, comfort and predictable days, weeks, and schedules. Let them go. Maybe you told yourself that life is supposed to be this way – miserable at times so you can be happy at other times – and you married that theory in a match made in hell. Let that go, too.

In those honest dialogues when you are really scared, truly vulnerable, and even clueless in some ways, you will know that you are willing to start over if only it means to stop the lying – I know I did.

So, are you being honest with yourself? How honest – all the way? What do you want in life? What do you want to be, do, have? And what, if anything, are you doing about it?

Chapter Three

R-e-v-e-r-s-e the Choices

The quality of our lives is determined by the choices we make: which career path we take, which partner we choose, the lifestyle we embrace. Just as you have the responsibility and the power to make choices about your wardrobe, your relationships or the car you drive, you have the same responsibility and power to choose your attitude and approach to life.

One psychology theory research suggests that we all have a happiness "set-point" that largely determines our overall well-being. We oscillate around this set point, becoming happier when something positive happens or the opposite, afterwards returning to equilibrium. But this set-point, to a certain extent, can be reset. Although our general mood levels and well-being are partially determined by factors like genetics and upbringing, roughly forty percent of our happiness is within our control, according to some experts, and a large body of research in the field of positive psychology has shown that happiness is a choice that anyone can make. As psychologist William James put it, "The greatest discovery of any generation is that a human can alter his life by altering his attitude."

With that said, a great day starts with you. This mantra is what I speak since I've started this journey. Early on, I noticed how quickly I gravitate more often towards positive things. I'm a huge fan of positive stories told by humble, like-minded people. I worship God, the One who created the sun, moon, and stars, which radiate and represents all positive things. The sun burns inside my soul. The stars allow only a glimpse into the mysteries of the unknown, and the moonlight shows nothing is so far away that it is unattainable. By no means am I perfect, mistakes are forever a part of my DNA. Right and wrong and pessimistic vs. optimistic are daily struggles just like good against evil. A miscalculated decision can cause one heck of a domino effect and will send you going backward rather than forward.

Finally, I learned the value of freedom, not so much in the physical sense but mental. While in my version of a mental holding cell, I began to drift off in various directions such as what it might feel like having a successful career, traveling all over the world sharing my story on stages. I could imagine the crowd applauding and the energy being electrifying as I walked out to stand in the midst of my supporters and captivate my listeners within ear range just from the sound of my voice.

I've discovered since my transformation, the inner peace that has been lying dormant has surfaced. I don't see the glass as half empty; I see the glass as half full. I'm tested daily with a phone call, work, even myself; but as quickly as I can, I regroup, reroute my thoughts and practice my mental exercise, which is to visualize the glass of water, extract the seriousness from the situation, dig to the core and resolve it there. Trust me, it's not easy, and the more I encounter these things it's also not as hard as I once thought it was.

If you aren't happy or you desire something else, what is holding you back from changing your life circumstances? Are you afraid people will judge you for making a crazy decision? Or are you afraid you will fail, and people will laugh? Tell the truth. Only then can you make conscious choices for yourself. It's hard to decide when you are emotionally wrapped up in other people's opinions. Parents often lay heavy "should" on their children in the name of protection. Friends, colleagues, and strangers often drown out the voice in your heart. I have met people who didn't know what they really wanted to do with their life or didn't have the courage to follow their desires until they spent half, or all, of their careers doing something else. You might start your career down one path and decide you don't like it anymore, but you have financial obligations that keep you from moving on. Your sense of obligation keeps you from exploring what really matters to you, what you now enjoy, and what would be fulfilling to you in your next phase.

Often "should-motivated" people become resentful and fatigued because they are constantly doing what they think they have to do rather than what they choose or want to do. "Shoulds" are so pervasive it is no wonder people are dissatisfied and disappointed at work. They often blame their bosses and the company for their resentment. They rarely blame their own fears. So, they live their lives in compliance and spend their time either complaining or dazing out. Is this you?

Choice means you are free to do or not do something because you decided on your own. To activate conscious choice, you first have to do some work to determine what really matters to you. What strengths are you proud of? What tasks do you most enjoy? What dreams keep haunting you? What would you do if you had no obligations or people to please? Take time to sort through your desires. Then answer these questions: What do you think others will say about you if you choose to make a change? Write these statements down so you can separate them from your own feelings.

If you extracted the opinions and shut out the judgments, what is left? Can you find a way to take at least one small step toward your desire? Each step could help you feel more confident. How can the situation be reframed so the choice that feels uncomfortable is considered on par with the easy way out? What are merits of the uncomfortable option? If you decide not to take the uncomfortable path for now, at least you made the choice for yourself.

The recognition of your should-based actions and the practice of personal choice can lead you to a should-free life. A life that is moving forward and not in reverse.

Chapter Four

Illegally Parked

Sometimes things don't go as we planned regardless of how well we plan. When this happens, we are tempted to give up and label ourselves a failure. That inner voice starts to remind you of its warning for you not to step out on faith. It brings to your remembrance how things were at least predictable when you were living your old life, before you started on this journey of living in your purpose, on purpose. Yes, that inner voice gets louder and drowns out all words of encouragement and motivation to continue going.

Everyone wants to be a success. I have never met anyone who purposely set out to be a failure. Undoubtedly, this is why so much has been written on the topic "How to be a Success" and why such books are so popular. I believe it was Theodore Roosevelt who said, "The only man who never makes a mistake is the man who never does anything." The simple reality is that failure is one of those ugly truths of life—a common experience to all of us to some degree. Thus, the ability to handle failure in its various forms and degrees is a vital part of the spiritual life and another sign of maturity. A careful study of the Bible reveals that most of the great figures of Scripture experienced failure at one time or another, yet those letdowns did not keep them from effective service for God and operating in the purpose. As a partial list, this was true of Abraham, Moses, Elijah, David, and Peter. Though they failed at some point, and often in significant ways, they not only recovered from their failure, but they used it as a tool of growth— they learned from their failure, confessed it to God, and were often able to be used in even mightier ways.

The way a person meets his own failure will have a significant effect on his future. One would have been justified in concluding that Peter's failure in the judgment hall had forever slammed the door on leadership in Christ's kingdom. Instead, the depth of his repentance and the reality of his love for Christ reopened the door of opportunity to a yet wider sphere of service. "Where sin abounded, grace did much more abound."

A study of Bible characters reveals that most of those who made history were men who failed at some point, and some of them drastically, but who refused to continue lying in the dust. Their very failure and repentance secured them for a more plentiful conception of the grace of God. They learned to know Him as the God of the second chance to His children who had failed Him—and third chance, too.

The historian Froude wrote, "The worth of a man must be measured by his life, not by his failure under a singular and peculiar trial. Peter the apostle, though forewarned, three times denied the Master on the first alarm of danger; yet the Master, who knew his nature in its strength and in its infirmity, chose him." Understanding the amazing grace of God and His incredible forgiveness and acceptance through

Christ, a mature Christian is one who has grasped the truth that his or her failure is not the end of an effective life with and for the Lord. While there may be consequences to live with (as with David) and serious issues to work through, the mature believer rests in the grace of God and uses the failure as a backdoor to success through growth and understanding.

"Who will separate us from the love of Christ? Will trouble, or distress, or persecution, or famine, or nakedness, or danger, or death? *36* As it is written, "For your sake we encounter death all day long; we were considered as sheep to be slaughtered." *37* No, in all these things we have complete victory through him who loved us. *38* For I am convinced that neither death nor life, nor angels, nor rulers, nor things that are present, nor things to come, nor powers, *39* nor height, nor depth, nor anything else in creation will be able to separate us from the love of God in Christ Jesus our Lord (Rom. 8:35-39).

In view of this, we often speak of the victorious Christian life. But the truth is there is a lot of defeat in the Christian's life because none of us will always and perfectly appropriate the victory over sin that Christ has accomplished for us by the cross. Further, the amount of deliverance we each experience is a matter of growth; so, on the road to maturity and even after reaching a certain degree of spiritual maturity, Christians will fail—sometimes seriously so. We don't like to talk about it or admit it, but there is a lot of failure. Failure is a fact of life for Christians, but God's grace is more than adequate to overcome any situation. The mature Christian is one who has learned to apply God's grace remedy for failure.

The Prevailing Attitude About Failure

Presently the bookstores are full of popular "How to Succeed Manuals" on every conceivable subject. And why is that? Too often, it is because we look at failure with eyes of scorn. We view failure as a Waterloo. We see it as the plague of plagues and as the worst thing that could happen to us. Thus, the fear of failure has many people in neutral or paralyzed or playing the game of cover up. We consciously, or subconsciously, ignore our disappointments because to admit them is to admit failure and that's a plague worse than death. People often refuse to tackle a job or take on a responsibility for fear of failure. People believe if they fail, they are no good. They think failure means you are a bad person, and you are a failure. But, as previously mentioned, most of the great leaders in Scripture at some time in their careers experienced some sort of failure.

For instance:

- When Abraham should have stayed in the land and trusted the Lord, he fled to Egypt because of the drought. And this was by no means the last of Abraham's failures.
- Moses, in trying to help his people, ran ahead of the Lord and killed the Egyptian. Later, against the command of God, he struck the rock in his anger.
- When David should have been out in the field of battle, he stayed home and committed adultery with Bathsheba and then plotted the murder of her husband.

- Peter, despite his self-confidence and his great boast, denied the Lord, as did the rest of the disciples who fled before the evening our Lord's arrest was over.

There is a fundamental principle here. Sometimes God must engineer failure in us before He can bring about success with us. Our failures are often steps on the ladder of growth—if we will learn from our mistakes rather than lay in the dirt. This is not to make excuses for depravity or to place a premium on mistakes or failure. This does not mean that a person must fail before they can be a success, but our failures, whether in the form of rebellion or just foolish blunders, can become tools of learning and steppingstones to success. The point is, we should never allow our fear of failure to paralyze us from tackling a job or trying something that challenges our comfort zone. More importantly, we should never allow failure to persuade us to give up. Nor should we allow past failures to keep us down or keep us from recovering and moving on. This means we should never allow failure to make us think we are a failure or that we can never change or that we can never again walk in purpose, or that God can't do anything with us because we have failed in some way. The Bible says we are all sinners and prone to failure, but in Christ we can become overcomers.

After the horrible carnage and Confederate retreat at Gettysburg, General Robert E. Lee wrote this to Jefferson Davis, president of the Confederacy: "We must expect reverses, even defeats. They are sent to teach us wisdom and prudence, to call forth greater energies, and to prevent our falling into greater disasters."

Mature Attitudes About Failure and Success

(1) Mature believers understand that a Christian can become successful despite failure because of God's incredible grace and forgiveness. We may have to live with the

results of some of our failures, yet God is free to continue to love us in Christ and use us for His purposes because of grace.

(2) The mature believer seeks to use failures as lessons for growth and change. Mature believers will act on two principles: (a) They understand that failures remind us of the weight and subsequent consequences of certain decisions. Failures remind us of what can happen, they can make us careful, but they should not be allowed to paralyze us. (b) The mature believer recognizes that our failures show us what we should and should not do; they become lessons in where we went wrong and why. You know what they say, "hindsight is 20/20." It can help us avoid the same mistake twice if we will learn from history.

Thomas Edison invented the microphone, the phonograph, the incandescent light, the storage battery, talking movies, and more than a thousand other things. It was December 1914, and he had worked for ten years on a storage battery.

This had greatly strained his finances. One evening, spontaneous combustion had broken out in the film room. Within minutes, all the packing compounds, celluloid for records and film, and other flammable goods were in flames. Fire companies from eight surrounding towns arrived, but the heat was so intense and the water pressure so low, that the attempt to douse the flames was unsuccessful. Everything was destroyed. Edison was 67.

With all his assets going up in smoke (although the damage exceeded two million dollars, the buildings were only insured for $238,000 because they were made of concrete and thought to be fireproof), would his spirit be broken? The inventor's 24-year old son, Charles, searched frantically for his father. He finally found him, calmly watching the fire, his face glowing in the reflection, his white hair blowing in the wind. "My heart ached for him," said Charles. "He was 67—no longer a young man—and everything was going up in flames. When he saw me, he shouted, 'Charles, where's your mother?'

When I told him I didn't know, he said, 'Find her. Bring her here. She will never see anything like this as long as she lives.'" The next morning, Edison looked at the ruins and said, "There is great value in disaster. All our mistakes are burned up. Thank God we can start anew." Three weeks after the fire, Edison managed to deliver the first phonograph. (3) When mature believers fail they:

-Acknowledge their failures and refuse to hide behind any lame duck excuses.

-Study or examine what happened so they can learn from the failure.

-Put it behind them and move ahead.

Being assured of God's forgiveness, we are to put our failures behind us, count on and rest in His assurance, and refuse to use them as an excuse for morbid introspection, pessimism, self-pity, depression, and fear of moving on.

(4) Mature believers grow through failure. They will know and act on certain truths:

- We are accepted in the Lord based on Grace, not our performance.
- We are human and, thus, we are not now perfect, nor will we ever be. God still has a plan for our lives.
- God is not through with us yet, and we need to get on with His plan.

(5) The mature believer will be one who understands there are different kinds of failure. There are those who have genuinely failed per the principles of Scripture. If we fail to know why we believe what we believe and then fail to give an adequate reason to those who ask for a reason for our hope (1 Pet. 3:15), then we have failed in our responsibility to witness. That can become a steppingstone to getting equipped and to becoming bold in our witness, but at that point there was failure. There is a false guilt of failure because of a wrong view of success.

There is another class of failure; those who mistakenly believe they are successes! These people may earn an honest living and be fine supporters of the church. They unconsciously (or sometimes all too consciously) consider themselves examples for others to follow. Yet they do not realize that from God's perspective they are failures. One man put it this way: "I climbed the ladder of success only to discover that my ladder was leaning against the wrong wall!" Heaven, I believe, will be filled with surprises. Many "successful" Christians will be nobodies, and some whose lives were sprinkled with the wreckage of one failure after another will be great in the kingdom.

(6) The mature believer is one who understands the importance of choosing the right standard of measurement to determine success and failure. There are several common beliefs about success that people apply to themselves and others, but they are all distortions of the truth. Most of these are based on some form of faulty comparison.

Fundamentally, this is the distortion of comparing ourselves with others. We are all to do our best according to the abilities God has given us, and we are right in using others as models of Christ-like character. Paul told the Corinthians, "Be imitators of me as I also am of Christ" (1 Cor. 11:1). But this is not the same as when we compare ourselves with other people from the standpoint of their gifts, abilities, bank accounts, possessions, position and other such standards and then attempt to determine our success or failure or that of someone else based on such comparisons. If money is a basis of judging success or failure, it is obvious that Jesus Christ was a failure. Consider this: when He had to pay taxes, He asked Peter to find a coin in a fish's mouth. Why? He didn't have a coin of His own. Christ was born under the shelter of a stable's roof. Most of us would be appalled if our children could not be born in a modern hospital. When He died, the soldiers cast lots for His garment. That was all He owned of this world's goods. He died naked, in the presence of bystanders.

Was Christ a failure? Yes, if money is the standard by which He is judged. The foxes have holes, the birds of the air have nests, but the Son of man did not have a place He could call home. Of course, earning money (and even saving some) is both legitimate and necessary. But the amount we earn is not a barometer of God's blessing. And I might add, lots of money and things are never an evidence of success in God's eyes. Many who are wealthy are failures from God's viewpoint. The point, then, is the absence or presence of money is not in itself proof of success or failure. The comparison game reaches out to almost every area of life. It may involve comparing friends, i.e., name-dropping to suggest that one is successful because he runs with the right people. None of these things are in themselves a proof of success in God's eyes.

All failure teaches us the important truth of just how desperately we need God and His mercy and grace in our lives. Sometimes our failures are mirrors of reproof, but always they can become tools for growth and deeper levels of trust and commitment to God if we will respond to them as such rather than rebel and become hardened through the difficulty. God is adequate for all kinds of failure. Some failures may not be our fault, but they serve as reminders that we must live with eternal priorities in mind.

In closing, I want to share with you a story I read. The story was about a man who was the sole survivor of a shipwreck who was stranded on a small desert island with only the items from his ship that had washed up on the shore with him. The man carefully constructed a small hut to store his few precious belongings and to protect himself from the weather. One day as he was standing in the ocean fishing for his next meal, he turned back to shore to see that his hut was on fire with smoke billowing into the air. The worst was happening. "God, how could you do this to me," he cried. He believed that all was lost. Later he heard an approaching ship in the distance. It was coming to rescue him. "How did you know I was here?" asked the man of his rescuers. "We saw your smoke signal," they replied.

"Destiny is a mysterious thing, sometimes enfolding a miracle in a leaky basket of catastrophe." – Francisco Goldman

When things in life go wrong we often fall apart, stress out, or get depressed and sad – yet in that very moment if we could step back and consider that maybe, just maybe, the hard time we are going through right now is really just leading us to the most amazing situation we could ever imagine, and what lies ahead in this new situation is going to bring us success beyond measure – if we could just trust that God truly does have a grand design for our life and that everything we are going through is meant to help us, to prepare us, to teach us, and to lead us to a situation that will create the very best outcome possible for our life – maybe then we would have the courage, strength, and fortitude to get through those tough times with a level of endurance and a hope for the future that will help us pass through those times more quickly and without so much sadness. Maybe then we could live each day feeling happy and grateful for what we are learning today and with hope for what tomorrow will bring.

***

"Your journey has molded you for the greater good. It was exactly what it needed to be. Don`t think you`ve lost time. It took each and every situation you have encountered to bring you to the now. And now is right on time." – Asha Tyson

Chapter Five

The D-Word

You will not be able to live on purpose, and in your purpose, if you have the wrong people around you. These people are called DISTRACTIONS.

Sometimes the wrong person isn't the one you are romantically linked to. Sometimes the wrong person can be an immediate family member. Whatever the case, you cannot afford to be attached to people who pose an imminent threat to you living the life God purposed for you to live. You must arrive at a place within yourself where you have no qualms saying farewell to those who are no longer going in the same direction as you. The reality is, toxic and unhealthy relationships and the drama they bring, cause more damage than anything else. These types of relationships are like a cancer that infuses its way into your destiny and slowly begins to chip away at it. You may not notice a difference instantly, and you may even brush it off opting to deal with it later; but before long you will find yourself wondering what happened to your drive, your motivation, your faith, and your belief that you are were born and created for something magnificent. You will know you are in good company if the company you keep is constantly pushing you to greatness and challenging you to be better even if you think you have already made it. The wrong company will do the exact opposite and cause you to question the things you know God has said about you.

Here is the first takeaway point of this chapter:

Everybody is not going to like you. You got that? I need that to settle into the fissures of your spirit. No matter how fascinating you may believe you are, some people just won't find you enthralling. Some people are going to find fault in everything you do. For some people, you will never be enough, and nothing you do will be good enough. There will be people who will love being around you if you are not a threat to their little kingdom. They will like you if they feel better and bigger than you. But, once God begins to bless you with something, they wish they had, then the problems ensue. And that is okay. That's not your problem to be concerned with. If you want everybody to like you then you are pretty going to have to resolve to not going anywhere and not having anything. More people are not living their life of purpose because they are more concerned with what others are thinking about them, or not thinking about them. You will never get anywhere in life if you are waiting for everyone to join hands with you and help you get where you are trying to go. There must be a built-in determination that drives you even if you must go alone. Despite the naysayers, you must keep going towards the goal line. And, you know what, as I kept going, God sent people who every now and then jumped on the field to offer a towel, a word of encouragement, and even a push when I felt like giving up. When you are living on purpose those are the type of people it is imperative you be surrounded by.

The definition of the word friend varies from person to person, and depending on that person, it's possible for them to have a distorted view as to what it means to be a friend. There was a time when being referred to as someone's friend meant something. Nowadays, you should be extremely mindful of who you consider a friend. In our society, your "friend" may be "friends" with your enemy. Loyalty is scarce among friendships today, thus the reason you should be more concerned with finding individuals who are associated to your purpose. Those who are connected to your purpose don't take the connection lightly, and they don't take you for granted.

Destiny partners are those who are divinely sent by God to help you live in your purpose. They are the ones who are not intimidated by the visions God gives you and aren't behind the scenes secretly wishing for your downfall. They aren't the ones who are vying for a position in your life, they are there to help you carry out an assignment. Purpose partners may not hang out with you on the weekends. They may not come over for holiday dinners. They may not sit in the box with you at sporting events, but they are there when it's time to do something in conjunction with your purpose. These are the people who are willing to jump in where needed and even if they don't get public recognition for the work they do, they remain faithful to their purpose which is to serve your purpose. And in today's times that is huge because there are people who live to see how many likes they can get on Facebook, double taps they can get on Instagram, and retweets on Twitter.

Second takeaway point:

Find your destiny partners. One of my favorite Biblical examples of Purpose Partners is that of David and Jonathan. The Bible reads in I Samuel 18:1-4, "After David had finished talking with Saul, Jonathan became one in spirit with David, and he loved him as himself. From that day Saul kept David with him and did not let him return home to his family. And Jonathan made a covenant with David because he loved him as himself. Jonathan took off the robe he was wearing and gave it to David, along with his tunic, and even his sword, his bow and his belt."

Identifying Destiny Partners

Destiny partners are linked to your spirit. The scripture says Jonathan became one in spirit with David. It's great to have friends, but friends may not necessarily be linked to your spirit. Don't believe me? Do something that a friend isn't fond of and see if that thing will withstand the test of the friendship. You can be friends with someone today—hanging out at the mall, shopping, dining—and fall out of that same friendship by nightfall. Friends will walk away. Friends may decide they don't need you anymore, but Purpose Partners are joined to your spirit with spiritual ties that are stronger than fleshly ties and aren't easily broken. It is tremendously easier to remove someone from your life than it is removing them from your spirit. Thereby, if a purpose partner is linked to your spirit, whatever is conceived in your spirit (purpose related), they are immediately attached to it and will ensure that you give birth to it. Their only question is, "How can I help?"

Destiny partners will take risks with you even if it puts them at risk. David and Jonathan were what we would consider today best friends. Jonathan was so knitted to David's purpose that he was willing to risk his own life if necessary. Jonathan went against his own father, King Saul, and told David, whatever he needed him to do, he would do it. (Read I Samuel 20: 1-42) Don't miss the dynamics of this. Saul, who was initially fond of David, eventually loathed, and his own son, Jonathan, was willing to lose his life so that David's life could be spared. Do you have any people in your life who are willing to delay, let alone give up, their own dreams, goals, and desires to make sure your purposed is fulfilled? Not only was Jonathan willing to risk his life, but he also came up with a plan to save his life. Let that marinate. A Destiny Partner will help you strategize so you can identify the many options that are available for you to be successful. Imagine if a football team only had one coach and that coach was responsible for designing plays, calling plays, and watching the field to make sure the plays were executed. There would be a lot fewer people gunning to be coaches if that much pressure was on their shoulders. Such as the same for a person with purpose. A lot less people would be willing to live in their purpose, no matter how much they may want to, if they had to do everything alone.

Third takeaway point: YOU CAN'T DO IT BY YOURSELF. A Destiny partner gets in the huddle with you and helps you strategize for the win even if they don't get the praise for it. What is a coach without a defensive or offensive coordinator? What is a purpose without Destiny Partners?

Destiny partners are givers. When Jonathan made the decision to be in covenant with David, the scripture says he took off his robe, his tunic, his sword, bow, belt. Wow, what a gesture to make. Most of us have trouble getting people to spend a dollar with our new business, let alone make a sacrifice to give us what we need even if they themselves need it. It is for certain Jonathan could have replaced those garments and weapons, but the notable thing here is that he took it off immediately upon seeing the need and gave it away. Destiny Partners don't wait to think about if they are going to give, they give to the cause right away void of hesitation. I believe it is safe to assume Jonathan's robe and tunic were crafted and stitched with the most expensive fabrics and threads. He was the son of the King. This would be equivalent to a woman giving away her brand-new Louis Vuitton bag or a man giving away his brand-new pair of Jordan's. Not too likely to happen. However, there was no reluctance in him taking it off and handing it over. He did it with joy and gladness. Why? Because he was in covenant—because he was linked to David's purpose. Purpose Partners have an innate desire to see you have all you need to be effective in your purpose. Even if it delays their gratification.

My friends, you cannot fulfill purpose without Destiny partners. It is time for you to do an evaluation of the people in your circle. It is time to say goodbye to anyone who isn't contributing positively to your life. No book, Pastor, preacher, teacher, or life coach can convince you to do this until you get to a point where the relationship is no longer worth it if it means sacrificing another moment of your destiny. When God is going to do something new in your life, whether it be going to the next level of your destiny, bring Destiny Partners on board, or taking you into a season of prosperity; God will often lead you to a place where cuts must take place. The same way everybody cannot make the basketball team, everyone can't go with you all the way.

That is my final takeaway point of this chapter:

Everybody can't go. When God was going to do something in Moses' life, He called him to the back side of the desert. When Jacob was at the point of change in his life, he found himself alone wrestling with God. Everybody will not be able to go where God is going to take you. Everybody will not be able to hear what God is about to speak to you. Everybody will not be able to see what God is about to show you. Some people will not be able to handle the blessings and prosperity God is about to give you. Therefore, God is taking you to a place where the crowd cannot follow. Where the doubters will have no room. Where the haters are irrelevant. The cuts are necessary because is positioning you for greater and if you are not careful people will mess you up. You can't blame the devil for what you can handle yourself. It's time to rid yourself of the people who subtract but don't add. Those who divide but do not multiply. Such folks will slow your progress and hinder you from getting where you need to be, when you need to be there. If they can't handle what God is doing, they are not your Destiny partners and they need to GO. Now. Keep in mind that the closer Jesus got to the cross, more and more people began to lie on Him, persecute Him, and forsake Him. Even some of His disciples.

When Joseph was born, his brothers had no problem with him. It wasn't until they realized he was their father's favorite when their father gave Joseph the coat of many colors, did they become full of jealousy and envy. Matters grew worse when Joseph began to share his dreams with them. They couldn't handle it and perhaps one of the reasons was because they themselves didn't have a vision or a dream. Some people have no issues with you until you decide that being average no longer suits you and your desire is to be great. Destiny partners will be elated by that declaration. They are eager to celebrate and rejoice with you. They are fulfilled when they are invited to the victory celebration. They are elated when the promotion comes. Why? Because a win for you is a win for the entire time team.

Beloved, you must resolve that your purpose is not attached to anyone who is willing to walk away from you. If they walk away, I will admonish you to host a going away party. You don't need anyone in your life that can easily walk away. Do not beg people to stay in your life. Do not beg people to be your friend or care about you. Stop trying to force people to share your dreams and visions. No matter their relation to you, what your history with them might be, or what they have done for you in the past; if they need to go, then in as many languages as you know, you need to wish them goodbye. The Bible says in, I John 2:19, "They went out from us, but they were not of us; for if they had been of us, they would no doubt have continued with us: but they went out, that they might be made manifest that they were not all of us." Destiny partners walk on the same level with you. They have the same spirit as you. They DO NOT walk away. I love how Bishop T. D. Jakes says, "The gift of goodbye is the 10th spiritual gift."

To receive all God has for you, to live on purpose, you need to be in the proper position, and surrounded by the right people. People who may have started with you but are no longer with you may not necessarily be bad people. It just signifies their part of your story has concluded which means you need to stop trying to extend their presence. Ever been watching a movie and a scene goes on and on and on? Isn't it irritating that you are forced to wait for the scene to end before a new scene can be introduced? Nothing will bore me more than watching a movie that is slow to build or change scenes. So, the same way you wouldn't want to watch a boring movie, why would you continue trying to hold on to the person who clearly wants, and needs to go?

Always remember that the enemy's most successful entry point into the life of a believer is through another person. So, guard your world. Guard your purpose. While Jesus preached to the multitudes, he had seventy disciples, twelve of the seventy were considered His chosen, and only three were truly a part of his inner circle. Destiny Partners don't always consist of many people, but they are always the chosen people.

Chapter Six

Stuck in Neutral

Once you discover what your purpose is the next thing you must do is start living it.

I know you're thinking that is easier said than done, but if you don't decide to do it, you will eventually fall into a doubt trap that will entangle you in procrastination. Before long, months will have passed, and the next thing you know, it will be years later, and you will still be talking about what you are going to do versus doing it.

What if the time isn't right? What if living on purpose requires you to abandon your current way of thinking, your current way of living, or your current way of surviving? Those are all questions commonly asked by individuals who are vacillating with the idea of making a move towards living on purpose. Let me ask you this. What do you have to lose? If you are not living on purpose, chances are you are unhappy anyway, and what is your happiness worth to you?

You may have noticed that as you get older, time seems to move faster. Summers are shorter, you often run behind, and spend more time than ever before catching up. No matter how we perceive the passing of time, the fact is, that the clock is ticking. Every moment that you don't get started, is a moment that passes you by. This is not to say you should always be busy, but isn't it time to stop waiting for the perfect time?

If you aren't ready to get started, figure out what is holding you back from taking the first step. Fear of failure? Fear of looking silly? Laziness? Depression? What could be scarier than living a life that passed you by? What could be worse than going day to day feeling uninspired, unmotivated, and stuck. Feeling silly, facing fear, and being a little crazy will help you choose to change. Admit it, embrace it, fix it and move forward. This is the right time, your perfect moment to start living life on purpose.

So, let's talk about fear—the ultimate purpose blocker. Fear is the most powerful single factor that deprives you of being able to achieve your full potential. You experience it most often because of your own thoughts and emotional visions, rather than actual real-world causes. In other words, you become fearful of a fantasy – something that doesn't exist.

Fear is a cloaked enemy that whispers negative thoughts into your mind, body and soul. It tries to convince you that you will not succeed and that you cannot achieve your full potential. These thoughts are lies.

The road you are traveling may be a bit scary at times, but don't lose faith. Don't listen to your fears and the fears of those around you. Don't let old setbacks work their way into your present thinking. And most of all, don't give up on what's important to you. It's fine to feel a bit uncomfortable. It's okay if you don't know exactly what's going to happen next, or how much you can handle. If you gradually step forward, you will learn what you need to know. You will let go of the scary things that 'might happen' and start to see all the great realities unfolding around you. This is your life and it's an open road. Grab the wheel with both hands and keep steering yourself around all the unnecessary fears and uncertainties as they arise.

Here's how:

1. Envision and declare what you want. Regardless of fear or actual real-world barriers, whenever you want to achieve something, you must envision it and declare it. You must keep your eyes open and focused specifically on what you want. It's simply impossible to hit a target you haven't declared or get anywhere worthwhile with your eyes closed and your vision blurred. The first step is realizing that what you want to achieve is already a big part of who you are. You may be a novice just beginning a great journey, or you may be a veteran who hasn't yet realized her dream. Either way, the fact that you haven't attained your desired result yet doesn't make you any less of a force to be reckoned with. In other words, if you want to run a marathon, you are a

marathon runner. You just need to run. If you want to be a writer, you are a writer. You just need to write. It's only ever a matter of training, studying and practicing. Whatever it is you want to do, envision it and declare it out loud: "I am going to _____."

2. Know the consequence staying where you are. What would life be if we had no courage to attempt anything? It wouldn't be. Life is movement. Inaction based on fear not only stops you from achieving, but it also stops you from living. Your future depends on what you do today. The fear of failure, or whatever, can be daunting, but it's nowhere near as bad as the realization of looking back on great opportunities you never took. Don't be satisfied with telling stories others have lived. Write your own story, your way.

3. Believe. What you believe either weakens you or makes you stronger. If you want to give yourself the best gift you could ever receive, believe in yourself. The foundation of the success you desire is not based on being in a

certain place, at a certain level of achievement, or a combination of external factors; it is simply a mindset. Success is an attitude that comes from powerful beliefs and empowering thoughts. What you think and believe about your life directly determines how you feel, what actions you take, and what you ultimately achieve. Believing takes practice, but it also makes the impossible possible. Is it worth the effort? Absolutely!

4. Take it slow but FAITH it! Yes, take a step, and another. Keep going! Achievement involves lots of doing. What you achieve is based on what you believe AND what you act upon, not just what you believe. You've got to take your beliefs and put persistent effort into them. There is no progress without action. What is not started today is never finished by tomorrow. Some of the greatest ideas and dreams die young. Why? Because the genius behind the idea or dream fails to FAITH forward with it – they think about it, but never DO anything about it. Just remember, no action always results in a 100% failure rate. So, get into action now and

begin moving in the right direction. After you get started every step thereafter gets easier and easier, until what once had seemed light years away is suddenly standing right in front of you.

5. Accept that failure is possible and necessary. As Winston Churchill once said, "Success is stumbling from failure to failure with no loss of enthusiasm." Failure is necessary. On the path toward success, you may encounter many failures, but YOU are NOT a failure. Failures are simply steppingstones that slowly uncover the correct path forward, one slippery step at a time. You can't get anywhere without these steps. So, don't wake up at eighty years of age sighing over what you should have tried but didn't because you were scared to fail. Just do it and be willing to fail and learn along the way. Very few people get it right on the first shot. In fact, most people fail to get it right on the first twenty shots. If what you did today didn't turn out as you had hoped, tomorrow is a new opportunity to try again and build upon what you've learned. And remember, in the end the greatest thing about

your journey is not so much where you stand at any given time, as it is about what direction you're moving. Your fears are not as scary as you think, and they're not here to stop you. They're here to let you know that what you want is worth fighting for.

One of the most majestic of all creatures is the tiger. For many years, these big, beautiful creatures have puzzled researchers. It seems that when tigers hunt, they have a remarkable capacity for causing their prey to paralyze with fear, a capacity greater than any of the other big cats. As the tiger charges toward its ill-fated prey, it lets out a spine-chilling roar. You'd think this would be enough to cause the prey to turn and run for its life, but instead it often freezes and soon becomes the tiger's food.

At the turn of this century, scientists at the Fauna Communication Research Institute in North Carolina, discovered why you're likely to freeze rather than run when a tiger charges. When the tiger roars, it lets out sound waves that are audible – the ones that sound terrifying – and it also lets out sound at a frequency so low you can't hear it, but you can feel it. And so, as the tiger emerges from the undergrowth the flashing of its colors, the sound of its roar and the impact of the unheard, but felt, sound waves combine to provide an all-out assault on your senses. The effect is you are momentarily paralyzed, so even though there may be time to avoid the tiger, you are tricked into standing still long enough for the tiger to leap on you.

Our fears often operate in the same way. They paralyze us into inactivity, even when the real threat is not immediately upon us. Part of overcoming the challenges before us is to recognize the ability for our fear of what might happen to stop us from dealing with the challenge. So, how do we deal with fear when you are trying to live on purpose?

Let's look at a couple of ways:

Feel

Our first point of recognizing the emotion, is seeing where the physiological changes occur within our body. Note where in the body you are feeling a reaction, "I'm feeling tightness in my chest". From there, observe the voices in your head, what are you thinking? From there, label what emotion you are feeling "I am feeling tightness in my chest. I had the thought that I can't do this." Then breathe. Take a few deep breathes leaning into the fear. Soothing your soul. Calming your mind. Breathe into the fear.

Elevate

Get bigger than your fear! When we are in the midst of having an emotion our body language changes. We feel fear, we turn inward, hunching over, crossing legs protecting ourselves from the perceived threat. Therefore, you must do whatever needs to be done to counteract that feeling. Clap your hands. Stomp your feet. Be bigger than the fear voice inside.

Action

As Nike would say, "Just do it!" Move forward in life, push through the resistance, and do the task you fear the most. Create new evidence that you can do things that are a success. Note all the good things in your life, all your achievements and all the positive things you have already created. Take note of the fear and push through. Do what you fear the most. Only then can you grow and learn as a human being. Only then can you step into your light and own your power!

Respond

Be kind to yourself. Speak with loving words. Understand where your fear is coming from and what you are believing about yourself to be the truth. Loving yourself heals. Compassion changes both yourself and those around you.

It can be a scary thing chasing your dreams. The fear of leaving behind what you have always known to embrace the unknown. When we push through fear, we shred old beliefs, destroy past patterns and change limiting thoughts. Feel the fear and move forward anyway. Acknowledge it, lean into the physiological responses, breathe deeply, and go for it. At the end of the day see yourself as a scared little child seeking reassurance and comfort. Provide yourself with loving compassion and firmly say, "We are going to do this."

Faith, as you may know, is the antidote to fear. Sometimes the only way to discover God's will is to practice stepping out and finding out. If I have prayed about a situation and don't seem to know what I should do, I take a step of faith. I know that trusting God is like standing before the automatic door at the grocery store. You can stand and look at the door all day long, but it will remain closed until you take a step forward and trigger the mechanism that opens the door. Don't spend your life in so much fear of making a mistake that you never do anything. Scripture says, "For God has not given us a spirit of fear, but of power and of love and of a sound mind" (2 Tim. 1:7, NKJV). You cannot drive a parked car. You need to be moving if you want God to show you which way to go. He leads one step at a time. If you take one step forward in the wrong direction, He will let you know before you go too far.

I often think of Joshua, a man who was given a huge task by God – one I'm sure he didn't feel ready for. Can you imagine how he felt when Moses died, and God told him that he was going to take over and lead Israel into the Promised Land? Fortunately, God knew Joshua was up to the task. In Joshua 1:6, the Lord commanded him: Be strong (confident) and of good courage, for you shall cause this people to inherit the land which I swore to their fathers to give them. That day, Joshua had a choice. He could step out in faith and watch the Lord do the impossible through him...or he could stay in his "safety zone" and never find out. Instead of being afraid of new things, you and I ought to be excited about the new challenges and opportunities that God brings into our lives. Even when everybody else tells us it's impossible, if we will step out in faith like Joshua and follow God, He will give us the grace to go forward.

I've certainly made my share of mistakes over the years. But through all of this, I learned a valuable lesson: When we step out in obedience to God while we feel afraid, then that releases the grace (or power) of God to do what needs to be done. It is unbelievable what God can do if you'll fight your way through all the opposition that comes against you and say, "If God says I can, I can." It's important to remember that when the Lord calls us to do something, He also gives us the motivation and energy to press on through each challenge that comes.

Maybe you're thinking, Yeah, I've missed a lot in my life because I was afraid to step out or fearful of what others might think. You know what? I believe God has you reading this for a reason. You can't change the past, but you can begin today to follow your heart and step into the things God has for your life. Sure, there will be obstacles, and sometimes you will make mistakes. But you must be true to what God's calling you to do if you want to be happy.

Friends, I encourage you to find and live in God's purpose for your life. Find what's going to fulfill you and all you're meant to be. Then choose to be bold enough to step out into an amazing, memorable, life-changing journey. When you step out into the unknown to do what you believe is God's will, He may not give you an exact blueprint to work with, but He will guide you step-by-step all along the way.

On the following pages I want you to write the things you fear as it pertains to living on, and in, your purpose. After you write your fears, I want you to look at the objectively and find the reason for your fear. Then, write down ways you can conquer your fear.

_____

_____

_____

_____

_____

_____

_____

_____

_____

_____

_____

_____

Chapter Seven

The F-Word (focus)

The enemy's primary FOCUS is to get you to lose your own. He will use a failure, a disappointment, or a letdown to try and convince you that you are possibly on the wrong path and need to turn your attention elsewhere. He knows that if he can take your focus, he stands a good chance of getting you to abandon your purpose, too. As we talked about in the last chapter, a failure doesn't constitute the end. It may mean a restart. But it certainly doesn't mean things are over.

It has proven to be very difficult to remain focused during distress or discontentment. Sometimes, no matter how hard you try, you get distracted from pursuing God's purpose for your life. Not to mention that every now and then the goals you once held near and dear seemingly slips from your grasp? You can have a purpose that begins so clear and distinct only for it to later become blurry and nondescript. It is vital to your purpose for you to maintain your focus at all costs, and yes, even when things don't go your way.

Elijah sort of had this problem in 1 Kings 19. He had just won a great victory for God in the contest on Mt. Carmel, but instead of being hailed as a hero and welcomed by the people of Israel, Jezebel sought to kill him. Discouraged, Elijah fled the country and seems to have decided that he could not go on anymore. This was also Jonah's problem. He did not want to preach repentance to the people of Nineveh, because he did not want those people even to have a remote chance of being spared from God's destruction. Jonah wanted God to destroy Ninevah. When they repented, Jonah was upset. He went out and sat himself under a vine and pouted, angry that God's way was not his way.

Also, the experience of having tried hard but not having seen very much tangible results for one's work in their purpose causes some people to lose their zeal for that work and to cut back on their work for the Lord. Maybe it has been the work of teaching, or the work of service to others, or the work of trying to encourage other Christians. If a person works long and hard and sees very little reward for their efforts, it is probably only natural to want to give up and let someone else do the frustrating work. If you have lost your zeal – however it may have happened – how do you get it back? The answer is simple: you get it back in the very same way you got it in the first place.

A frustrated New York attorney sits across from the "other woman," pleading for peace. He attempts to make restitution, to justify his one-night stand, to say something--anything--that will get this obsessed woman to leave him, his possessions, and his family alone. But with cool deliberation, she simply replies, "I will not be ignored." Though secular, this scene from a 1987 film contains spiritual significance. The woman, obsessed in the pursuit of someone else's husband, is completely focused on her immoral mission.

How much more focused should we be in pursuing our divine destinies? For this character, only death could stop her. What is stopping you?

While this woman had a fatal attraction, many Christians today suffer from fatal distractions. Fatal distractions detour us from growing spiritually and fulfilling our purpose in life. And while it is easy to list the many external diversions that cause us to lose focus--busy schedules, difficult people, lack of money—the disturbing reality is simply this: Our most fatal distraction lives within.

It's the person you see as you brush your teeth, the one who stares at you in the mirrored glass of corporate America, and the one who goes with you to pick the kids up after school. It's even the person who accompanies you to the office, and the one who intercedes in times of intense warfare.

As the 1950s-political cartoon character Pogo stated: "We have met the enemy, and it is us."

Often our fatal distractions are rooted in our minds. What else would explain King Saul's fatal distraction, the jealousy of his armor bearer,

David? When the two returned from battling Goliath, women praised the war effort in song, saying, "'Saul has slain his thousands, and David his ten thousands.'" (1 Sam. 18:7, NKJV). It was at that moment that Saul allowed the seed of distraction to awaken in his mind." Then Saul was very angry, and the saying displeased him; and he said, 'They have ascribed to David ten thousands, and to me they have ascribed only thousands. Now what more can he have but the kingdom? So, Saul [jealously] eyed David from that day forward" (1 Sam. 18:8-9).

Like so many of us, Saul's fatal distraction did not come from external forces. It wasn't the women, David, or even the lyrics of the song. Saul's jealousy was his fatal distraction, and it caused him to disqualify himself from serving as king. Saul is the only one who could have changed this negative thought process, and the same is true of us. If we do not truly believe what God has said about us, fatal distractions will come to weed out our faith.

Just Faith It! Fadrienne Jones

What is distracting you from seeing yourself in the reflection and image of Christ? Is it doubt, a poor self-concept or lack of intimacy with Christ? What do you believe about yourself? What do you believe about your potential? Beyond your scripted, religious response to friends or family, what do you truly believe about your service? As Proverbs 23:7 declares, "For as he thinks in his heart, so is he."

If you've been fatally distracted, there is hope. God wants you to regain your focus and pursue His original plan and purpose for your life. To do that, you must stay faithful to the things of God and obey His Word. Stay committed to the call of God on your life, be unshaken in your faith and remain steadfast in your Christian walk.

Like the woman with the fatal attraction, like the Canaanite woman mentioned earlier, aggressively pursue your destiny. Instead of being fatally distracted, stay eternally focused on fulfilling His will. If you tend to obsess over what is NOT working, you're not alone. We're drawn to place our attention on what isn't working in hopes to get rid of the problem. However, the more time you spend thinking about your failure or problem, the worse you'll feel about yourself and the less time you'll have to devise a solution.

When things go wrong, ask yourself the following two questions:

1.   What have I learned about myself / my career / my business?

2.   What can I do today to avoid the same result in the future?

The answers to these questions will help you shift to problem-solving mode. And that is precisely what I would like for you to do right now. Yes, right now. I want you to follow these steps so you can regain your focus (if you've lost it or are losing it). Maybe you are yet to encounter distractions, in which case, you can skip to the next chapter. But for those who have had issues with staying focused, the following practical tips will you help you realign with the zeal you once had for living on purpose.

1. Give yourself permission to succeed. If you haven't truly given yourself permission to enjoy success, you'll be placing roadblocks along your path to lifelong achievement. It is easy to become distracted when you haven't committed to achieving your goals with both your head and your heart.

2. Decide what is important to you. Have you noticed that you always seem to stay focused on those things that are most meaningful to you? If you're not staying focused on the task at hand, it may be time to reprioritize what is important.

3. Write goals that motivate to you. Do your goals motivate you? If not, it is imperative that you rethink your goals.

4. Develop a workable plan of action. It's easy to become distracted when you don't have a well thought out plan of action. It is worth taking the time to write out a month-to-month plan for achieving your long-term and short-term goals. It's also worth the time to write an effective and reasonable daily to-do list – a list that will help

you remain focused on going forward one bite-sized piece at a time.

5. Be accountable. Find an accountability partner. Find someone who is willing to check in with you and support your progress. Research shows that you'll probably accomplish more if you have someone with whom you are accountable.

Your purpose is what you can't live without and what can't live without you. You have something to contribute. The "little things" shouldn't be allowed to get in the way of it. A vision has kept people alive through the harshest of conditions and driven others to the peak of greatness. With a clear picture of your destination, all levels of goals suddenly become more possible and within closer reach. A good vision helps you weed out the things that don't fit in the picture. Remember that our lives are not stagnant as we are always shifting and changing. So, make it a daily practice to review, re-organize (if necessary), and you will be sure you are always moving forward decisively. Remember, your circumstances today are a direct result of your past thoughts and beliefs, which direct your actions, which creates a certain result. If you start thinking and acting in a different way today, you will create different results tomorrow.

What is your plan to avoid distraction?

_____

_____

_____

_____

_____

_____

_____

_____

_____

_____

_____

_____

_____

_____

_____

_____

_____

_____

Chapter Eight

JUST FAITH IT!

C an you recall the first time you heard about Santa Claus? Do you remember the excitement you felt each Christmas season as you anticipated this oversized man with the big belly and white beard stuffing himself in your chimney to bring you toys? Most of us didn't even have a chimney attached to our house, but we bought into the myth because in our childhood state we were expert dreamers. We had the ability to travel to faraway places in our imagination. This was proven by our belief in childhood stories such as: Cinderella, Beauty & the Beast, Sleeping Beauty, Jack & the Beanstalk, Snow White & the Seven Dwarfs, Pinocchio, and the mystical Peter Pan. We looked forward to allowing our imagination to run wild through the forests right alongside Little Red Riding Hood, and I think we have all at some point pretended to eat some porridge in the chair next to Goldilocks. It was something so innocent and dare I say it— magical—about the innocent landscape of our mind as children.

When we got older that mystical element of our juvenile imagination graduated to a more mature phase that we have termed daydreaming. When I was a teenager, I would sit with my friends for hours talking and daydreaming about what I was going to buy myself when I got older, or how sweet life was going to be when I finally got out of my momma's house. Anybody remember doing that? If you were like me, you already knew what type of car you were going to drive, what type of house you were going to live in, what your husband's or wife's last name was going to be, all the way down to what you were going to name your kids. It was fun to sit and imagine these things because they gave us something to look forward to as we transitioned into adulthood.

But then, we got older and something happened. Something knocked the wind from underneath our imagination and stripped away our ability to daydream. What used to be all fun and games turned into a borderline torturous experience each time we attempted to have the audacity to hope and believe.

Well, I can tell you exactly what happened.

Life happened.

Hopes fizzled into disappointments. Dreams became nightmares as one thing after another happened, and instead of taking the time to dream, you turned your focus to merely surviving. You started existing in life because that was easier than trying to live in purpose. It was less stressful to settle into monotony and mediocracy because at least there you knew what to expect. At least you could manage your organized chaos, and whatever happened from there would either be a plus or a minus—hopefully a plus.

I know what it feels like to take up residence in complacency and have absolutely no expectation of anyone or anything. With expectation comes potential heartbreak so you spare yourself the possibility of feeling any more pain than you already have and wish for the best outcome possible. But, my friends, that is no way to live. It certainly is not how you live on purpose.

Honestly, I'm not sure most people know how to dream anymore. Many of us seem to drift along, never dreaming, never longing for something better, never fighting to achieve, and never following the power of a single purpose. I am not referring primarily to getting things – new cars, new homes, the latest Apple gadget, and the like. We have garages full of things, but still lack a single, compelling purpose for living. Without that purpose, we drift along as sticks in a swollen river. Think about many of the people you know. Many are after things that do not seem to matter much. They feel that life is composed of the accumulation of gadgets and devices. But if that is all life is, then life is nothing worth contending for.

To have a purpose in life is a guiding and steadying influence. What you are "up to" in life is one way of describing your purpose in life. Another way is to think about what you consider .

most worthwhile. These are the same way of asking, "Why are you living?" "What is your purpose in life?" We simply must have some overall purpose in life. Joseph Addison said, "The grand essentials to happiness in this life are something to do, something to love, and something to hope for." Those elements give us a reason to get up in the morning and to keep pursuing our dreams even when they seem out of reach. We are made to live on purpose and to live on purpose you must not be void of expectation.

People with a clear-cut sense of purpose can withstand many challenges, inconveniences, and difficulties that others cannot. They do not give up. These people are like the explorer Ballard who kept going for 13 years while pursuing his dream of discovering the Titanic. People who live on purpose are like the early travelers who risked their very lives to carve out places in the wilderness for their families.

One person's mountain is another's molehill. The same hammer that tempers steel shatters glass. The difference is in the material.

Thus, it is with life. An experience that might throw one person off course is hardly even an inconvenience to another. One is drifting and gets sidetracked anywhere. The other knows where he or she is headed and lets nothing interfere for long.

To live on purpose does not mean to barrel headlong through life so intensely that you miss life while trying to live. Some of life's greatest moments come as surprises that are happy opportunities that seem to signal, "Hey, wake up. Pay attention. Be in the moment." Someone has wisely observed, "Life is not measured by the number of breaths we take but by the places and moments that take our breath away."

I read of an experiment that demonstrates the difference between existing by chance and living on purpose. Processionary caterpillars feed on pine needles. They move through the trees in a long procession, one leading, the others following, each with its eyes half-closed and his head snugly fitted against the rear brim of its predecessor. The French naturalist, Jean-Henri Fabre, after patiently experimenting with a group of these caterpillars finally enticed them onto the rim of a flowerpot. He succeeded in getting the first one connected with the last one, thus forming a complete circle, which started moving around in procession with neither a beginning nor an end. Fabre expected that after a while they would catch on to the joke, get tired of the useless march, and start off in a new direction.

But they didn't. Instead, the living, creeping circle kept moving around the rim of the pot. Around and around, keeping the same relentless pace for seven days and seven nights until they died of exhaustion and starvation. Food was close by, but was outside the range of the circle, so the caterpillars continued along the comfortable path.

People can be like that, mistaking activity for accomplishment and movement for direction. We can follow habit to oblivion. We can be so resistant to change that we perish. If we are going nowhere, we will get there soon. In the same manner, we get what we expect to have. And to get something you never had, you must do something you've never done or quit doing due to exhaustion or disappointment.

Expectancy is the close cousin to faith. And, you know without faith it is impossible to please God. I know you think you are playing it safe when it comes to living a life without expectation, but you are also cutting it close to displeasing God. Which would you rather do? Most have no problem expecting the unexpected in a negative sense. You have experienced those moods where everything has gone wrong that could go wrong. At these moments, you have all the faith in the world in Murphy's law that "If anything can go wrong, it will go wrong." It is no trouble at all to believe that the next disaster that is going to happen is that the sky is going to fall, or the roof is going to cave in. When it happens, you say, "I told you so. I knew it was going to happen. I knew the worst was yet to come." Looking back on those situations, you may even begin to believe that there is something prophetic about your ability to predict the unpredictable. It is easy to be "a prophet of gloom and doom". After all we expect Satan to do the unexpected to make our lives unbearable. Too often, we don't expect God to do the unexpected and redeem us from the unbearable circumstances.

God moves based on our faith. We want God to do the unexpected, but we don't expect him too. We know that with God all things are possible, but do we believe they are probable? Our prayers are intense, but we have little expectation. Our faith is so rooted in earthly circumstances we are unable to look up and see the handiwork of God. When God does the unexpected, we have difficulty believing what God is doing. When God answers prayer in an unexpected way, we often struggle to identify his answer.

Every time I take a flight I think about the force of the work behind the scenes that is taking place to bring the aircraft to its intended destination while passengers are seated comfortably in their seats. That same thing is taking place in eternity to ensure our safe arrival in heaven as we speak, only it is on a much more impressive scale. Angels are being directed, heaven and earth is being moved in unexpected ways to accomplish God's will in our lives. God and his heavenly host are working around the clock making sure that everything conforms to the purpose of his will so that he may be glorified through his work in us.

The story is told of a small town in which there were no liquor stores. Eventually, however, a nightclub was built right on Main Street. Members of one of the churches in the area were so disturbed that they conducted several all-night prayer meetings and asked the Lord to burn down that den of iniquity. Lightning struck the tavern a short time later, and it was destroyed by fire. The owner, knowing how the church people had prayed, sued them for the damages. His attorney claimed that their prayers had caused the loss. The congregation, on the other hand, hired a lawyer and fought the charges. After much deliberation, the judge declared, "It's the opinion of this court that wherever the guilt may lie, the tavern keeper is the one who really believes in prayer while the church members do not!"

When we expect great things from God, there will always be those who think we are out of our minds. We are far from being out of our minds when we expect to experience great things as God unfolds his comprehensive plan bit by bit and piece by piece before our very eyes throughout our entire lives.

What is your expectation for the future?

Are you trusting God's plan?

I want to challenge you to see it before you see it. It's okay, go ahead and believe God for greater. Did you know God has expectations to? It's written in His word in Jeremiah 29:11, "For I know the plans I have for you," declares the Lord, "plans to prosper you and not to harm you, plans to give you an expected end."

Your Heavenly Father wants to upgrade you! So, stop sitting back and taking whatever life throws at you. Dust off your dreams. Dust off your vision. Dust off your goals. I believe that he is going to do exceeding, abundantly, above all you could ever ask or think of Him to do. (Ephesians 3:20) Who wouldn't want that? Yes, I know you've had some difficult hardships. I know life for you may not have been a crystal stare, but there is still hope. As sure as there is life, there is hope. Start daydreaming again. Get that childlike excitement back just as you had when you knew "Santa Claus" was coming. I know it was disappointing when you found out Santa Claus wasn't real, but I've got someone much better to recommend to you. Your Heavenly Father. He may not be sliding down chimneys, but He is seated on the right hand of the Father making intercession for you, and all you have to do is delight yourself in Him, and He will give you the desires of your heart! (Psalm 37:4)

Get reacquainted with your dreams. Write them below and allow yourself to JUST FAITH IT!

Made in the USA
Columbia, SC
07 October 2024

43215257R00065